GROWING
THE
SPARKS

HOW TO BRING BACK THE *'SPARKS'* AND THE *'MAGIC'* IN YOUR LOVE RELATIONSHIP

PAUL McLOVETT

LasGEORGES
PUBLICATIONS

COPYRIGHT

DEDICATION

This is dedicated to my lovely, most beautiful and gorgeous wife

FOREWORD

M ark met June years ago at a college function and immediately they fell in love. It began as a simple likeness fuelled by a passion to what seemed to be a never-ending romantic story. The random tantalizing massages by the fireplace, the nostalgic breakfast in bed moments, the never ending texting throughout the day and calling just to say 'I Love You', these were the moments that defined this deep love they had for each other.

Both Mark and June could not help but praise each other wherever they went and the profile pictures on their Twitter and Facebook pages constantly had a photo of the two of them smiling, giggling looking all time happy. Their friends even acknowledged the deep desire the couple had for each other. "You make the perfect couple", 'You look smashing together", and I think you found the one"...the compliments were pouring out wherever they went.

It is hard to believe it is the same head-over-heels-in-love couple who now sit far apart in the living room not speaking to each other. Every morning is painted with pictures of self-independence; everyone makes their own coffee, no more holding the door for the other to pass, the constant texting and in-boxing reduced to two word messages or none at all. "He's fine" or "She is doing okay" become the popular answers whenever friends inquire about their wellbeing.

...Where did the love go?

Many of us find ourselves in this position. It is like love wears two masks; at one, part we are happy and content with each other, but somewhere along the road the fire dies to a struggling flicker. What happened? Where did we go wrong? Is there a way to fix this?

As we, all already know that Love is the most profound emotion known to human beings. And for most of us the most meaningful element of our lives is having a loving, romantic relationship. The unfortunate thing is that, the ability to have a healthy, loving, romantic lasting relationship is not innate.

In many cases, almost all of us have experienced a failed relationship, and most of us have to work consciously to master the skills necessary to make them flourish. But, the good news is that with effort and perseverance, on our part, we can learn what we need to know to make our relationship work, placing it on the loving, romantic and long lasting "till death do us path". Without doubt, there are big problems that afflict relationships; and it is sad to say that these problems which include infidelity, abuse, irritations, bad tempers and addiction are not going extinct from the earth. Although we live in a highly sexualized society that constantly bombards us with an alluring sound of distractions from everywhere, and no one is immune to it.

But most of the times it may be the petty problems that most covertly subvert love in many relationship. Like, the way our partner chews so loudly. The dirty socks on the floor, Like the relentless drip of a leaky faucet, the snoring in the nights, little irritations, they often time erode the goodwill that underlies all relationships. And before we know it, that feeling of being unloved, unappreciated, and unheard start to creep in and gradually an intimate loving relationship becomes a pale memory.

Over the years relationship experts and psychologists have concluded that the main challenge in a relationship is "figuring out how to negotiate and live with your partner's irritants in a way that does not alienate them and keeps the two of you connected." Most relationships fail because the partners are fighting, not over big issues but petty differences in their opinion, point of view and style.

What you will learn in this book is what I learnt in the last 29 years of my marriage and in my experience counselling young and old couples in the local community, who go through troubled times in their relationship. Carol and I had learnt a lot about relationship before we met and when we first started together we applied a lot of what we learnt and we still keep on learning. It's not all been rosy but with dedication and commitment the sparks keep on growing and the light of romance has never dimmed.

My insights and advice are based on my own personal experience from helping thousands of couples understand how to make the commitment to grow a lasting rewarding romantic relationship full of passion and sparks. If you apply what you will learn in this book you will see great improvement in your relationship, your partner will be more committed to building a lasting love life with you and you will see yourself loving more of yourself, and your partner as your love grows one day at a time. But I should warn you that results may vary from couple to couple - so I encourage you to read my book with an open mind and decide for yourself if my insight is applicable to your situation and if it can help you.

Many couples write to me all the time about the amazing changes they're finally experiencing as a result of my materials and counselling. I truly hope they work for you, too. I would like to congratulate you on taking this powerful step to create a better future for yourself and your partner, and to cultivate, nurture and grow a long lasting loving, romantic relationship with bright sparks.

All my love

Paul McLovett.

INTRODUCTION

The Sparks and The Butterflies

*W*e can all remember when we first began dating our spouses; it felt like the butterflies were never going to stop flying. And for most relationship, the frequency of butterflies may dwindle at some point but it usually continued and even got stronger when it progressed to courtship. Then we got engaged and they increased as we walked around hand in hand with our fiancés excited about spending the rest of our lives with them.

In most cases, the honeymoon period seems to be the height of marital bliss. Those first few weeks, months, and years were some of the happiest for couples. For the newly married couples, arguments are few and compromise is very easy. Some few months and years into the marriage, reality kicks in; the two flesh are now becoming one as written in the bible. This is the period that responsibilities grow and you find yourself tested in ways that others who have gone through the road ahead said you would, but perhaps most of us don't think it would ever happen to us.

The birth of a child, redundancy at work, skyrocketing bills, issues from family on both sides and outside stresses from other sources can cause the butterflies in your stomach to cease to fly and the sparks that once filled your love relationship to gradually go out.

The main reasons couples lose the spark in their relationship vary for different relationships and sadly most people don't know how to get it back once it's gone out. Many couples try to do it the wrong way and they soon become frustrated from the failure and they eventually give up which further extinguishes the iota of spark left in the first instance.

The good news is that you do not need to panic when the relationship between you and your partner gets annoying or ho-hum. Getting the spark back into your relationship is perhaps simpler than you think if you would be ready to put in the little effort. When it seems that you already know the punch-lines to all his jokes, when you're seated in the restaurant with nothing to say or you never thought that you would be pretending to have headaches at bedtime. You definitely think the magic is gone.

What if getting the spark back between you and your partner doesn't require you to move mountains? But to take just some easy steps and actions that are guaranteed to bring back the butterflies and get the sparks going again.

Danny has been married now for over 4 and half years. At the time he got married to Lorraine he was madly in love with her. Over the 4.5 years they had two children who keep them busy all the time (ages 3 and 22 months). They both became so preoccupied with their children that it seemed like all they do was watch or clean up after the kids. Danny told me one day that the spark that he had over 4 years ago has gradually disappeared. "I just don't find myself wanting to be intimate with Lorraine and I would just rather be alone," he said to me. Danny is a saintly person without any questionable character; he does not cheat on his wife and he does not plan to do so. Besides, Danny is a strong believer in the institution of marriage; divorce being an option only in the extreme of circumstances. For Danny, divorce is not an option. All he wanted was to fall back in love with Lorraine again, but like most people, he did not know how to do it.

Does that sound familiar?

I worked with Danny and Loraine for a few weeks, and they both brought back the spark and the butterflies are soaring higher than ever before, they are madly in love again. Danny and Lorraine were willing to bring back the feeling they once had for each other and it was possible because they both put in the little effort it requires. In some cases, the effort is only need on the part of the partner who is losing or has lost the spark; the little effort I am talking about is directed towards yourself or your partner. In this book, I will discuss both cases in detail and I hope I will be able to help you see how easy it can be to re-ignite your love life and bring back the spark in yourself and your partner.

CHAPTER ONE

The 3 Long-Term Relationship Killers And How To Avoid Them

Focusing on the outside

*W*e must first establish that creating a long term relationship with a partner starts with creating a long term relationship with yourself.

For many relationships, the first three - six months are the best. Why? Because during this time your attention is on all the good things you appreciate about your partner and their attention is on all the good in you. Who wouldn't love that kind of romantic relationship?

But when you move in together with your partner and little things start to bother you, and if you're not aware of them or you have not made the commitment to working things out with your partner then that's when the three relationship "killers" begin to raise their ugly heads. They eat away at the love you once had for your partner until you can't even find that love anymore.

Here they are:

1. Blaming your partner

You hear words like "If you just weren't _____, then we'd have a great relationship."

And comments like these become preponderant between partners.... "Why don't you _____? You're destroying our relationship." "When will you _____?" and at some point the little ugly comments would deteriorate into this.... "I can't take this anymore."

You and I already know that blame is all about the other person. It's always their fault, if they'd just change, if they weren't so this or that, then you both would have a wonderful relationship. Like I said earlier, blaming is putting attention on all the things you don't like about your partner. Let me ask you one simple question... What do you think happens when you do that? The answer is very simple... You see more and more of their faults and the things that bother you about them. And the result you get is a daily torture and sooner or later the relationship just stops being fun.

2. Blaming yourself

"I'm not so good in certain things" "I'm a disaster when it comes to relationship." "I did not grow up with the kind of love I needed" "I can't give love because I did not receive it" "I was abused in my childhood" "It's `1234567`12

my entire fault, no wonder he/she doesn't want to be with me." "I'll never have the relationship I dream of."

People who direct blame at themselves are ashamed of themselves. Now, instead of blaming your partner, you're blaming you. Let's make no mistakes; blame is just as destructive, no matter who it's aimed at. When you see the worst in you, when you focus on all the wrong things about yourself, where do you think your partner's attention goes? That's right. It is focused on all the worst in you. You cannot create a long term loving relationship focusing on the worst things in you or in your partner.

3. Blaming Your Situation or circumstances

Have you ever said or heard some to the comments ..."Our current situation does not allow us to do what we should do" "We don't have enough money to be happy." "His work keeps him away so much we can't have a good romantic relationship." "He/she lives too far away for the relationship to work." "The people around you do not allow me to express my love as I love to". I have just quoted a few of the most frequent comments I hear from the couples I have worked with.

When you blame your circumstances, you are only justifying your inactions or wrong doings. What you're saying is if things were different, then the relationship could be wonderful. Again, just like focusing the blame on your partner or yourself, blaming your circumstance is a subtle way of putting attention on what you don't want and it's a highly potent long-term relationship destroyer. One thing I want to say about this is that all of these long-term relationship "destroyers" come from our cultural mindset of looking for solution outside of ourselves to make us happy and fulfilled in life. This is impossible in life and it's impossible in building lasting relationships.

HOW TO CREATE A HAPPY ROMANTIC RELATIONSHIP

Loving Yourself

L et me make this clear, Joy and Happiness only ever come from within. Do you want to have a great relationship? Create a great relationship with yourself. First build a long term loving relationship with who you are, YOU!

When you are in love with you, with who you are, how you show up in the world, your body, your mind, your soul, your passion, your style, your voice, your taste, when you love spending time with yourself, then a partner becomes an additional joy added to the joy you are already experiencing.

It is true that the right partner can help you through the tough spots. They can help you grow and overcome your own internal demons, but for that to be true, that relationship has to be based on what's right in each of you, not what's wrong. The great thing about loving yourself is your partner then becomes the one who reminds you of who you really are when things get tough. Your partner will encourage and nurture you when you are beating yourself up because they already know the stuffs that is in you.

4 Pillars of a Stable Long Term Relationship

1) *Looking inwards –*

This is the first law of love, love yourself first and then love others as you love yourself. This means you look to yourself for the love, the appreciation, the caring, the nurturing that makes for a fulfilling, lasting and loving relationship. If there are problems or obstacles, you look within for the solution and strength to deal with them. When you are able to do this, then whatever love your partner gives you becomes frosting on the cake of your own fulfilment. Looking inward for love and the solution does not mean you do not need your partner. It simply means you are not dependent on them for your happiness and fulfilment in life. From this place, your love for your partner can truly be unconditional. You want for them what they want for themselves. Then you will be able to give to others from what you already have, you will fulfil the law of love by giving love unconditionally.

2) *Focusing on the Gift* –

This is one of the most powerful ways to build a great relationship with anyone at any level. You consciously focus on the area of the gifts in your partner, see all that your partner is blessed with, everyone is gifted in one way or the other and I am not talking about the gift of singing or playing musical instrument. I'm talking about appreciating good things about your partner Rather than blaming them for things that bug you. When you play the Appreciation Game with your partner regularly, you will culture your ability to find the gifts that's in your partner.

3) *Commitment* –

Having a romantic relationship is like fulfilling the purpose of your existences. You will discover who you really are at the deepest level. Romantic relationships are for your growth. Because of this, anything that does not conform to the law of love will be healed by your commitment. So be committed, give your all, and give yourself totally. The amount of growth you experience in a relationship is directly proportional to your level of commitment.

It's been proven time and time again that the more committed we are to whatever we do, the more growth we see in it, and vice versa. But does that mean making a lifelong commitment is the key to a lasting loving romantic relationship?

How can you possibly know what you will feel or what will happen one year, two years, five years, ten years or 20 years from now? You can't. My simple answer to these questions about commitment is that you should be fully committed to your partner right now, in this moment. Is that possible? Yes! I know you agree with me it's possible. When you commit to this moment, then string those moments together for 10, 15, 20, 50 years, then maybe you will look back and say "that was a lifetime of commitment."

4) *Build rituals into your love life*

By this I mean have a well-organized schedule of your time and what you do but do not set them on stones. Rituals are the means to organize your time, your energy and your thinking. When you have a schedule to spend time together, you will build a habit of spending time together. And the habit will soon form a strong pillar on which your loving relationship will stand for ever.

It is through ritual that parents can spend time together, lovers can create ecstatic love-making, partners can resolve their challenges together. Structure ritual into your relationship so you and your partner get time alone on a regular basis, you have regular sessions to discuss challenges, you structure quality, loving time with your kids and you create a sacred space within which your relationship lives.

3 Powerful Love Games

*J*f you love playing games and you want to play games in your relationship, play these 3 games. I have taught these games to many of the couples that I have counselled and real life results have been phenomenon.

1) Appreciation Game –

in this game, each of you will look into your eyes, but it does not matter if you are sitting close or standing or taking a walk. Each of you take turns as you appreciate something about the other, and WHY you appreciate that about them. Mentions what you appreciate and tell your partner why that thing is so great about partner. It doesn't have to be many things; it could be just one thing, do not flatter, look into your partner and find the gift of God in them.

2) Gratitude Game –

This is a bit similar to the appreciation game, but this time you write down your diary, your notebook or somewhere in your smartphone the things you are grateful for in your own life and why you are grateful for them. This is like counting your blessings and giving gratitude for them. Do this at the end of every day. If it is just one thing that is OK, you will be surprise how blessed you are at the end of the week, the months and the year.

3)   *Thank God Game –*

This is a variation on the Gratitude Game and carol's favorite. You will say this to your partner "Thank God I met you... because..." "Thank God for..." "Thank God you are..." Take turns or make it a little competition to see who can find the most things to thank God for in the time allotted.

Always begin with "Thank God...."

These fun, simple games are simple rituals to consciously put your attention on the good in your life. Make that a habit and your relationships will become one more blessing in a wonderful life.

Find your higher-self, and begin living the life you were destined for.

By following this long-term relationship advice I gave above, Carol and I have been able to create a life of happiness with for ourselves and we live a life filled with passion and growing sparks in our love life. If you find you agree with my insight and you see them helping you in your own relationship, I encourage you to put everything into practice and I will be excited to hear about how your love life is changing for the better and how you are becoming more fulfilled and happy in yourself and your partner.

In the next chapters, I will be discussing some major and minor challenges that face many relationships today. No relationship is immune to these ugly incidences that ruin relationships and many marriages have collapsed because the partners involved ignored the warning signs and did nothing about it.

I will give you some real life examples and accounts from the couples I have worked with. We will discuss their challenges and interventions that gave them breakthrough to a more fulfilling, happy and long lasting love relationship.

CHAPTER FOUR

THE 7 MAJOR CHALLENGES OF LOVE RELATIONSHIP

Discover how to overcome them

THE TRUST

*F*or David and Rachel, love was always present in their marriage and they played a big role in the community they lived in. David was forever faithful to his wife and he never at one time thought of replacing her with anyone else. Rachel on the other hand trusted her husband and never had any reason to doubt him.

But the ugly happened, David had an affair with a woman and Rachel was unlucky enough to find out. David now beats himself up every day. On one session with me, he stated "I made a stupid mistake. I should not have made it in the first place". Like so many other victims of infidelity, David thought the grass was much greener on the other side. He lost the trust of his wife and this has definitely taken a huge toll on their relationship.

I once had a young man walk into my office and shared his concern and fear that his wife could be cheating on him. She received midnight calls which she never could give clear explanation to and she always concluded the confrontations with one sentence "It's nothing to worry about".

These two cases gave me great insight on how trust is structured in a relationship. It does not matter whether the actual act that leads to mistrust happens, but if a partner develops a feeling of doubt in believing in the other, trust is broken. To reignite a dying relationship, trust has to be present and alive.

Women by far are the greatest benefactors if their partners are trustworthy enough. If you show up home with lipstick on your shirt, it better be the same lipstick she left when she planted a morning kiss on you before you left for work. Your partner needs to feel that they trust you; that whenever you are out there they do not get feelings of insecurity because they fear you might be up to some mischief.

There are so many situations that would make a spouse doubt their better half. And if trust is shaken in the relationship, then the two couples need to reach a sense of reconciliation fast before everything breaks down.

It is possible to provide everything or anything your partner would wish for; big houses, flashy car, trips to exotic islands or abroad. However, if trust is compromised, then that relationship is bound to hit rock bottom. The worst part about trust is when it is not confronted or goes unresolved.

Mistrust is a number one killer in most relationships nowadays. The statistics are rising every day of happily married couples getting miserably divorced. Legal firms must be making booming business out of them, as the couples continue to wonder just what could have went wrong in the marriage.

It was all about the trust they had between them. You see, this virtue may seem to be so little but yet accounts for so many aspects that affect the relationship. If your wife says I trust you it means she is confident you will not try and flirt with your office mates or you will not be tempted to bank that fake cheque and fleece your client company of its money.

If a wife wins her husband's trust, the husband will never have to worry who comes to the house during the day, if she is a stay at home mum; or install a tracking device or plant a bug on her to monitor her movements. He doesn't have to check with her friends every time to see whether she is with them or follow her close whenever she excuses herself to pick a call.

I have noted amongst my many clients during sessions that the key issues always lead to trust. As one would expect them to be very different to each other, I will shock you by telling you that most cases of mistrust are quite similar and seem to arise from trivial issues. In most occasions, the element of mistrust has led to what relationship gurus call the deceptive behaviour; when one party discovers they cannot trust the other, they try to revenge against their spouse or get even with them.

However, it doesn't have to be an ugly end of the road for your relationship. It is better to identify all the possible reasons on how mistrust comes about which will be highlighted in the next page.

HOW TO REBUILD BROKEN TRUST

*O*ne day, I had a session with a female client; she was really distressed and took me a while to get her to sit down. What was her problem? Her husband had broken the trust she had for him and now she would not have any of it. As usual, I inquired more into the matter, trying to find out whether there were any traces of forgiveness and a willingness to resolve the matter.

She said one thing that I will never forget "Men are all the same". Then, I knew what the real problem was; she had been disappointed so often in past relationships that she now has difficulty trusting any man. Hence, every man that comes into relationship with her, she puts under radar. She is a victim of what I like to call past relationship syndrome. Many people have been through relationships where trust has been broken, and such people cannot see how the next relationship could be different.   Thus, they enter a relationship where trust is already an issue.

Some couples, in many occasions, I have discovered have low self-esteem issues. One person feels not good enough in the relationship or the other person is too domineering and demanding. In either case, one partner will often feel belittled and gradually their self-esteem is eroded away.

This could often leave the person with the fear of competition and dissatisfaction thus leaving room for mistrust to grow.

Such a person will tend to feel so low about themselves that they often form an opinion about everyone; they often feel that everyone just isn't whom they say they are. And that everyone is out on their way to harm them or do things that will break their trust.

A person may have grown up in a home where trust was an issue, for example, a child from a broken home, an abusive home or even a home where promises have been made and broken innumerable number of times. Such people I would classify as damaged goods and they would need to work on their lack of faith in the other person.

Trust is an essential ingredient for any relationship to last. It is a very vital building block. When there is no trust then it is time to rebuild it. To me, lost trust in a relationship is like a ticking time bomb that needs to be defused before it 'blows up'.

For David and Rachel, I advised David to try and work up the trust ladder once again. Good thing he did not get the 'order of the boot' nevertheless he still had a huge task of convincing the love of his life that he is still that guy she fell in love with from the beginning.

I advised David, to never again lie to his wife about anything and it will help him to always keep his wife informed about on his whereabouts. If he is heading to a specific place he would have to let his wife know; if he is going to make any pit stops on the way, she should know of that as well.

David would also have to learn not to sound defensive when answering sensitive questions, as this would always cause the alarm bells in his wife's head to go off.

Now if you still have the number to your secret lover, it is the best time to deal with it and break off association. Not every person out there is lucky to get a second chance especially when their spouse has caught them in the act. Keep the phone numbers or Facebook chats alive if you want to sign the divorce papers. It is time to let bygones be bygones and focus on your beloved one.

CHAPTER FIVE

THE COMMUNICATIONS

Never stop communicating to your partner

*I*n a great relationship, there are no sacred cows and no secrets. You talk about everything and anything.

You can express your mind, express how you feel and respect the feelings of your lover.

The heart of all relationship is in communication. If you get it right, you can live happily ever after, but get it wrong... break up may as well be knocking on your door. Nothing sets the fire of love, passion and romance in a relationship and leaves it burning for eternity than a couple who converse with each other. There is a huge difference between the husband who sits on the couch watching television while his wife talks and the man actively engages with his wife when she talks.

If we borrow a leaf from nature we would see animals always have a way of communicating to each other. Tiny hill ants bump into each other on their way, their antennas make contact and by this means they identify one another. Wolves making piercing howls at night are a way of gathering one another in a pack. Even whales have their own distinctive communication sound that can be heard miles away by those of its kind.

Nature itself teaches us that communication is important for wellbeing, thus we as human beings have an obligation to communicate.

Talking and listening are the only two components of communication. Everyone can talk but for communication to be effective, we all need to learn to listen too.

Women talk more than men in many relationships. Once more talking is quite free for the women while the men can be influenced and cultured to open up along the way. Women are by nature emotional beings and they find a great sense of fulfilment when they put out their thoughts. And when a woman speaks, a lot of feelings are engaged and in such moments she needs the most attention of her man.

When a man decides to speak, on the other hand, he does so because he sees a great importance in it, and he aims to achieve a particular goal through it. While it may not be much for emotional satisfaction, a man at such times may be searching for new avenues of ideas, advice or encouragement and approval.

Why is it that there is always free talk during the dating period but things change when the knots are tied and kids suddenly start to pop out? I cannot count the number of times I have heard the phrase "My husband just doesn't want to talk anymore, it's like I married a statue!" Or this one "I cannot tell what is wrong with her, she just keeps to herself and seems to be in a world of her own".

I have counted dozen cases of withdrawal by one spouse on the other and the relationship then sets for the rocks. I will share with you a particular case of Scott and June. These two began as the happiest boyfriend and girlfriend who delighted in each other's conversation. There just weren't enough words for them to express their feelings.

They no doubt explored every avenue of communication they could possibly think off; calls on their mobile phones and landlines, text messages, chats and messages via social media such as yahoo messenger and Facebook, emails you name it. Each chance they got to chat; they would talk and talk and talk and talk... But then a few years down the line the length of conversations and frequency began to dwindle and at some point even sending a text message became a struggle.

What is it about love that makes it start on a high only for it to hit a miserable low? It is like a song that starts with an energetic rock-metal hook but then slowly fades down to a sleepy country classic. As a romance and passion expert, I would say it has something to do with infatuation.

Infatuation could explain for all the words that we have for each other, words which seem to never end, no matter what we do. We are attracted to each other; we are so excited about each other we definitely want to learn everything we can about each other in seconds. This could explain the frenzy I have witnessed in speed dating; everyone is excited not because of the short time alone but infatuation plays an important role in getting the participants to literally rap about their life before moving onto the next speed table.

For the likes of Scott and June, I have always given this simple advice; Infatuation is not Intimacy. Infatuation is freely given while intimacy is earned. Communication has a big role to play in both spheres; that is in the infatuation stage and the intimacy stage.

The infatuation stage is where all illusions of love happen and we are guided to believe we have found the perfect one who we can never let go off. At the infatuation stage, all flaws are hidden and only the prime-cut traits are displayed in order to lure the partner in. The infatuation stage is where we do not see any fault in our better half and they just make us happy with every breath we take in.

The sad part about infatuation is that it is a temporary place to be. Just like the Northern Lights of Norway, Infatuation is a short lived feeling we chase for the entirety of our lives. We just don't want to let go of the 'in love' feeling because we believe it will be the end of our relationship. For some of us, we tend to think our partners don't love us anymore and we may at times take drastic measures like jumping ship and finding another person to love.

The sad reality is infatuation will end with the second person and you will find yourself hitting the road again. When the infatuation stage dies, it is dialogue that still sustains the relationship and which cultivates the feelings of intimacy. Which is why I echo the need of communication in every relationship, it leads both of you to the stage of intimacy.

Scott and June are a living example of how initiating communication once more could contribute to a healthy relationship. They both walked into my office one day casting souring grapes at each other. They just could not seem to have a peaceful dialogue with each other. Every conversation always seemed to end in a fight. According to the pair, this was a regular occurrence which often resulted in revenge silence lasting for days and sometimes weeks. So, on this day they had showed up in my office, they expressed fears that their relationship was at a tipping edge and anytime soon one of them might open Pandora's Box.

However, Pandora's Box still had some good left in it after all the vile stuff has been released to the world. As Scott and June's infatuation for one another began to cool down, they began to see the faults, dislikes and negatives of the other person.

Communication is important in sustaining any relationship beyond this phase. It is not enough just talking or speaking to each other; what you say, how you say it and the feelings you exude when talking all play a huge role in how effective communication is and this in turn shapes up the relationship.

Rule number one, when conversing with your partner, it pays a lot first to think about what you want to say before you say it. Whatever will come out of your mouth will it have a positive impact on the wife or girlfriend, boyfriend or husband? Experience with clients has shown me that it is not always a great idea to say stuff when you are angry.

Anger in communication is like poison in food. It completely distorts the entire message and may aggravate your better half. Words are just words; it is the emotions surrounding them that make the whole difference when it comes to communication. A husband who says 'You got to be kidding me!' with a cheerful and jovial face says something completely different when the same words are spoken in anger.

I tell couples when they come to me for counselling to always think of how they feel before they speak to the other person. When we speak we do not only communicate our words, our feelings are also transmitted unless we put our feelings to check. Know your feelings and you will prevent a whole lot of problems in your relationship. When you get into an argument with your better half, about 90% of the things you will be tempted to say will be hurtful. It works a whole lot better if you just took your jacket and went out for a stroll and come back when you feel fresh and cooled down.

Communication means clarity, and this is the quality of conversation you have with your partner. When expressing yourself, you have to make sure you have the words coming out clearly and they are making a positive impact.

The biggest give out to communication is how we express our feelings as well as how we project out the words we want to say. Non-verbal communication is said to contribute to a huge percentage of communication, which is to say, on many occasions communication is not just about the words but also about our body language.

Two people claiming to be in love and yet they stand a distance from each other says a lot about their relationship. Rival politicians showing up in the same conference, pretending to be friends yet they do not look at each other even though they are sat next to each other says a lot about them. A couple seated in a restaurant eating quietly and appearing to be more interested in other people in the environment rather than each other says a lot about them.

We have to learn to read the signs on our spouses' faces if we are to get a clear picture of what they are trying to communicate. If your wife says "She is fine" but you sense a sombre mood on her facial expressions, maybe she is telling you she wants you to prod further, and with love, in order for her to open up. If your husband comes home, doesn't give his usual greetings and proceeds to bed without doing dinner and still says "Everything is Ok", he is actually telling you that "I will talk about it when I think I am ready".

Reading the body language of your partner is one powerful way to communicate. It is good to master reading the tell-tale signs on the body posture, facial expressions, and hand movements to better understand the mood of the communication.

LISTENING IS NOT PASSIVE AND SPEAKING IS NOT ALWAYS ACTIVE

It is not uncommon to hear people complain that their partners do not listen to them. A typical day in a marriage relationship may be the wife laying out all her problems and concerns to the husband, while the husband is not paying rapt attention and even when he thinks he's heard her, he becomes a problem solver.

Trevor a good friend of mine was once in such a situation. Most mornings we attend the gym together. On this particular morning, he said to me "I don't think I am connecting that much with my wife these days."

You see, every time Trevor's wife gets on the couch to talk to talk about the issue of the day, Trevor cuts in in the middle of the conversation, he analyses what his wife is saying and begins to give a list of scenarios and solutions to what he thinks may be the problem. As this behaviour continued, his wife has now stopped talking to him.

Trevor loves to talk with his wife as it gives him a sense of connection to her. He loves to feel involved in what his wife is going through. But here lays the problem, Trevor was meant to offer a listening ear and only a listening ear alone. His wife, in all her talking was looking for a sympathizer and not a problem solver.

I explained to Trevor that what his wife was looking for is a listener not a problem solver. Women want their men to listen!

I advised Trevor to learn the art of active listening. He is to keep a comfortable and loving eye contact with her at all time and never let anything distract him at any point. In fact, to make the conversation more intimate, he can move closer to his wife and make gestures that show pure understanding and empathy with the wife's situation.

Trevor was only to speak when his advice is sought or when seeking clarification. He should pay attention the entire time. Trevor was not to fiddle at something, glance at any distracting element or start making a movement with his body as this could cause his attention to shift. He is to show genuine concern the whole time.

I advised him it was essential he maintained a relaxed posture and not present as though he would rather be somewhere else. He was also to pre-condition his mind to accept that he is there to listen and not try and be a Dr. Phil.

This might sound like a hard task to do for Trevor, but I like to say that for better results, all we have to do is just sit and listen like we do in the movies. When that great Iron Man Three movie premiered and you got the front ticket, you definitely did not have a conversation on your phone while you tried to catch the action all through. You just sat down, popcorn and soda in hand, watched and LISTENED!

Listening is not passive; it requires your attention and concentration to follow through with the speaker. A lot of the stress in relationship would be a lot less if men in particular would just learn the art of active listening.

DON'T STOP COMMUNICATING TO YOUR PARTNER

Communication is one of the vital languages that ignites the dying flicker and produces a fierce flame of passion and love. Husband and wife, boyfriend and girlfriend need to get into dialogue with each other. There is some sense of satisfaction when you share ideas with each other, when you get to know what each other is feeling and understand how best to act whenever those feelings are being portrayed.

There are several other avenues to increase conversation between the two people. I have always recommended to many of my clients to try and induce conversation in the bedroom. Instead of your bed being just for intercourse and slouching on after a long day, you can actually lay there together, cuddling and sharing each other's thoughts and emotions.

Some of the couples I work with often complain that they have no material they can bring up as conversation with their loved ones. This is not entirely true, yes we often find ourselves in this position but it does not mean we have nothing to say, we just don't recognize the many clues we get every day that give us avenues for dialogue.

Have you ever woken up and everything just doesn't seem to work right? You get to your car and it won't start and you have to leave it and take the bus to work. But the bus takes the route you always avoid because of traffic which means you waste time commuting only to get to work late. By the time you reach the metropolis, you already feel like you could have ran faster than the bus. During lunch break you make a quick dash to the bank, in hope of making a quick deposit, only to find this annoying long queue.

What were your feelings in such situation? I, often hear so many guys say they just don't have it in them to talk. The problem isn't that we don't want to talk, it's just that we are not conditioned to let out our feelings when need be. For some of us, some feelings are better off holding them in than letting them out.

Dialogue is important and you have a ready supply of it in how you deduce your surroundings and what feelings you get from such deduction.

CHAPTER SIX

THE EMOTIONS OF ANGER Vs COMPASSION

How to Deal With Anger Your In Relationship
Resolve any outstanding anger before bed time

*D*o not sleep until you've resolve any anger or misunderstanding, and do not let your anger affect your time in bed. Talk it through, resolve it, and give apology if necessary.

Nowadays most marriages and love relationships end after a repeated moaning and whimpering, not a bang. Many divorces and separations were not caused by too much anger, fighting, abuse or infidelity; rather, most relationships rupture slowly and die agonizing death from little or no compassion from partners.

Let me first talk about compassion;

Compassion

When another person huts and show signs of distress and you show sympathy, then you have shown compassion, you have shown that you care. Compassion acknowledges and appreciates, at heart, the simple basic human frailty inherent in all of us. Compassion makes you feel more human and makes you feel not isolated.

All of us need compassion for the formation of emotional bond to one another. Let me give an example: Think back to when you first met your lover, if you are now married, think about when you were newly dating; supposing one day you called your newly found love and you told your love that your parent had just died, if he or she responded with

"That's OK, please let me know when you get over it so we can go out or a meal."

You probably would not have fallen in love, married or still be with that person till today. We all fall in love probably with someone who cared and showed us compassion especially when we are feeling bad or on in bad situation. When compassion decreases in any relationship, resentment will rise and petty problems become insoluble and resentment can turn into contempt if not dealt with on time.

Anger

John and Diana were planning to go on vacation, but they did not agree on where, when and how much to spend on their vacation. At one point Diana made a suggestion expecting John to comment on her suggestion and John responded by looking at her, laughing and saying, "Are you serious?" it all started out as a small disagreement but it soon quickly escalated into a blowout.

And comments like "My feelings were hurt and I felt belittled," were said by Diana. The couple ended up not talking to each other for days and they slept in separate rooms.

Two of the many causes of ugly issues are anger and bad temperament. And it's sad to say that these are not perishing in relationships.

As you know that all of us have experienced the emotion of anger at some time in our lives, but most of do not know how to handle our anger because most people have never been taught how to deal with anger constructively. We have been programmed to think that if a person is angry the appropriate response is to seek revenge, which usually equates to violence. Instead of us to seek to k now why the person is behaving in the unpleasant way.

Interestingly, many researches have proven and validates that 96 to 98 percent of what people get angry about is rooted in childhood. According to Dr. Hegstrom "When people have been wounded they tend to gravitate toward and marry a person that they believe can fulfil the losses in their childhood," "For instance, a woman who grew up without a father might gravitate toward someone older and seemingly wiser whom she believes can help fill the void she is feeling. Or a man who was never listened to as a child might choose a mate that appears to be a good listener.

If someone does something to trigger your emotions about those childhood losses, you become angry at the person instead of you understanding what it is at the heart of your anger.

Lorraine becomes angry every time David arrives home late. She is irate and he doesn't understand why she makes a big deal out of his lateness even if he was late just a few minutes. David thinks Lorraine should understand there are many reasons that may cause anyone to arrive home late, but Lorraine was having none of it. This was a big issue. Looking back at Lorraine's childhood we find out that her parents divorced because her father was having an affair and would frequently come in late. Her anger stems from fear that David might do the same thing to her. And they have never sat down to discuss it. Anger is often a secondary reaction to a primary feeling.

Anger has been found to be one the major sources of stress in the family and people living with angry partners have been found to have high level of stress hormones. It is therefore very important to learn, recognise and understand how to resolve the emotion of anger, for the sake of health and happiness our the homes and relationships

4 Steps to Handle Anger In Your Relationship.

Be compassionate to your lover, learn to forgive and forget.

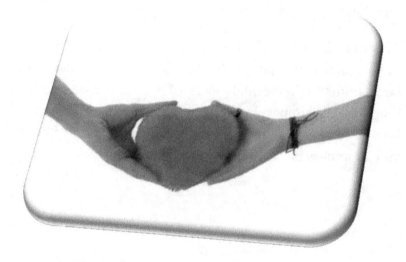

It is very crucial to remember that the person you love is a human being too. In times of challenge and disappointment, do your best to be compassionate and forgiving. It's impossible that your partner will always measure up to expectations. We all face challenges, stumble and fall. Showing compassion, help to your lover to overcome the challenge, be firm when it's necessary but be compassionate. The bible says one shall chase a thousand but 2 shall chase 10 thousand.

1. Identify the Source by looking back into your upbringing:

The first step in handling the emotion of anger is to identify how your parents or grandparents handle anger. Encourage your partner to think back to know what kind of losses they experienced in their childhood. If you are dealing with the anger yourself, think back and identify your losses. You will discover where the anger is coming from; you will find its root which may be feeling of hurt, neglect, abuse, invalidation, frustration, inadequacy, guilt, hopelessness, helplessness, betrayer, disappointment, fear, lack, discouragement etc. These are trigger points for anger. Every time someone pushes any of these buttons, the feeling of anger is elicited.

2. Deal with the source: by speaking to the trigger

Interestingly, psychologists have proven that one the best ways to deal with emotional problem is by talking to oneself when the emotion is triggered. Instead of always reacting with anger you can step back, hold your calm, take a time out and say, "I am to respond to what you said and this is how I will respond", "Is that what you meant?" When you start by asking your partner to first clarify what they said before you react, you delay what psychologists call 'the anger response processing zone (RPZ) '. You will be responding to issue positively in calm manner, your discussion would come to a logical conclusion and you and your partner will be happy.

3. Compassion:

Certainly, when the angry partner begins to deal with childhood issues they begin to grow and heal in these areas. And there is a need for compassion on the part of the other partner as it will take time to change. Many couples expect too much, too quick and too soon with little efforts. The good news is if a person is teachable all issues are fixable.

John and Diana were silent for some a period of time and at some point both of them looked at each other and said, "We need to settle this and move on."

According to Diana, the couple talked about their issues without raising their voices and without getting angry. When a couple have come to a point where they can discuss sensitive issues without yelling or raising their voices, the feeling is great.

4. Understanding and Forgiveness

Understanding why people do what they do will make forgiveness possible. You should seek to understand the emotional development of your spouse. When you fully understand that your partner's ugly emotions can be attributed to a scar in their past, you will be more forgiving and compassionate. You will be able to prevent strong heated arguments by the use of immediate forgiveness and compassion exercise.

A quick and intense expression of anger when there is a trigger can be damaging to any love relationship. Instead of giving in under emotional stress to the immediate expression of anger, inward expression of forgiveness and love will overcome the evil situation. If your partner gets angry you should always reflect inwardly say something like "I want to understand and forgive" or "I want to forgive and love" or "I chose to forgive and love" or "I will show compassion".

Continue until the anger decreases. Only after the angry feelings subside, should the spouse then communicate and open up the door to discussion. This quick movement to forgiveness is strengthened by the belief that the spouse is motivated to change their ugly behaviour.

Be in control of your emotions

When discussing sensitive issues and sacred cows, be civil, keep your emotions in check, do not let your emotions heat up and interfere with a good level headed discussion about sensitive issues. You will be able to talk openly about anything.

CHAPTER SEVEN

THE GRATITUDE

GIVING APPRECIATIONS

I once read a story of twin boys who were raised in two different foster settings. One twin was raised in a loving home, full of joy and thankful for everything that came their way. He was constantly praised when he did something good and was encouraged to do better when he failed. He grew up knowing the essence of appreciating people and he knew that by appreciating people he put a smile their faces.

The other twin on the other hand was raised in a family where achievements were not celebrated as success was the only expectation. Every success was only another door to another task to be accomplished. Failure was heavily frowned upon. This was a family where petty issues like talking about feelings didn't matter as it was considered a sign of weakness and life was all about conquering; even if it means stepping on others to achieve their goals.

Both boys became successful in life but the difference between the two boys was clear as we can imagine the quality of lives they each had. The first twin lived a happier life and was able to endow his family with the same love and affection he was shown as a child. The other twin as anyone would expect was top dog in his field. He had a string of conglomerates to his name. Unfortunately he could never build a lasting relationship with anyone as everyone he went into relationship with always felt they could never satisfy him and they seemed to be struggling to win his approval. He eventually got married to someone just like himself, who was more interested in success than touching lives.

Appreciation contributes to the feeling of fulfilment. It does not only enhance the life of the person being appreciated it also enhances the life of the appreciative person. Appreciation is such a small act of kindness but you have no idea the magnitude of impact it has. A husband needs to appreciate his wife and the wife her husband. Every day needs to be a day of appreciation; if she makes you a warm cup of coffee every day, you need to say thank you. If he mows the lawn and pays the bill you also need to say thank you.

The problem in today's world is that we rarely show gratitude for things we have or given to us. There is a lot of

'Thank You' at the beginning of courtship but somewhere down the line it fizzles out. We start treating acts of kindness like they were our rights instead of privileges. 'Thank Yous' are often now regarded as another 'See You Later'. No one really cares anymore.

Giving words of gratitude for things done to us all begins with the willingness of offering it. We have to make up our minds that we are going to do it; that we are going to start noticing actions done to us and we are going to be appreciative about it. I remember a nice couple I met when I was on holiday in the Caribbean Island.

Tamila and Rodney looked very happy and it was obvious to anyone who cared to look that they were enjoying each other's company dearly, running around like little children. I couldn't help but get the wife into conversation when her husband went off to take care of their lunch order. I asked her "How is it that there is still fire in your relationship? And what is your trick for keeping it burning?"

Her response was really interesting. She said that this had not always been the case with them. She reported there had been many years she now wished never existed. She remembered how her husband never used to appreciate her, how he just seemed to turn a blind eye to everything happening around him. She would re-decorate the room hoping her husband would notice but he would come home, take the remote and sit on his favorite side of the sofa and watch TV like nothing happened.

She reported that there were times when she would need him to help with the kids but he only made it his duty to remind her that it was a woman's job; after all, he brought home the bacon. She told me that this attitude from her husband always broke her heart and caused her to cry for nights wondering why he wouldn't just notice all that she does. She eventually reached her breaking point and he came home one day only to find a note waiting for him; she had left him and had also left the kids with him!

It was hard to believe that these two had been to that low point in their lives. "So how did you guys come back together?" I wanted to know more, and she must have something interesting to say.

He tried to pressure her back immediately as it seemed that he and the children were lost without her but she would not oblige him. After several months of separation he finally began to see things from her perspective and finally it dawned on him how ungrateful he had been and how he had taken his wife and kids for granted.

He sought her forgiveness, apologizing for all the years he had taken her for granted and undermining her role as wife and mother. He thanked her for putting up with male chauvinism and promised her he would never take her for granted again.

They have been back together 3 years now and true to his word he has not failed to appreciate her and he tries to seize every opportunity to show it and he gets the children involved too. Though Tamila did confirm that every now and again the old Rodney still pops his head out but that no longer mattered to her as she knows that he genuinely loves and appreciate her and all she does.

I will tell you the truth not many people out there can do that, but this has been perfect example on how important appreciation is in a relationship. We all need constant words of kindness and random acts of kindness to keep us going. We all need to feel appreciated, loved and know that we are always thought of and our actions or words are not taken for granted.

Like the husband here, we can start mending that broken link in our marriages or relationship only when we realize the importance of appreciation.

SHOWING IT IN A ROMATIC WAY

If you have seen the movie Evan Almighty, at some point you see God (Morgan Freeman) and Evan Baxter (Steve Carrell) having a conversation on what matters most in this life. God tells Evan that he should build an Ark every day; an Act of Random Kindness (ARK). In other words, this movie was teaching us about the important lesson of appreciation.

If you have never been that kind of person who offers kind words for free, how then can you begin to show gratitude to the beautiful woman or handsome young man you have in your life? Charity begins at home so kindness and appreciation also begins at home. Before you think of fancy restaurants or expensive gifts, how about using that one tool you have available with you at the moment; WORDS.

Number one, when you wake up every morning, look into the eyes of your lovely one, and tell them how much you love them. Keep the stare long enough for the words to sink into their minds and you can add some points to yourself and plant a loving kiss or a warm hug.

Two, try and note down all the things your partner has been doing in and around the house and you can start thanking and appreciating them for those things. Find a fresh piece of paper and write down the good deeds and just say how thankful you are. Leave the note by the bedside of your spouse or put it in their driver's seat before they leave for work. Such actions look so small but you have no idea the magnitude of impact they will have on the one you love.

Appreciation is a key ingredient in igniting love, romance and passion and every person in a relationship needs to feel appreciated. I know of a couple I worked with who now send romantic messages to each other. They always try to spice things up and they include a glass of champagne, a box of berries or a slice of cake as they enjoy each other. They did find that one thing that was needed to fuel their relationship; gratitude and appreciation.

In my years as a counsellor in both dating and marriage, I discovered one thing about appreciation, it's a feeling that you act upon without waiting. If you see that lovely necklace in the jewellery store and think of how good it would look on your wife, what do you do? Do you walk in and take out your wallet or just say you will get something like that next time?

Appreciation through action is not something you postpone, it is a burning desire to please someone you love and it is best served when it is hot. When you get those flowers from the local vendor before you walk up the steps to your house will not only put a smile on your wife's face; but you will also be rewarded with kind words and actions that would melt your heart out.

Here is another lesson about appreciation; when it burns in your heart and you wish to express it, then it doesn't matter how much you would be spending (this is not an excuse to break the bank...sorry). You cannot put a price on love. However, you must learn to live within your means. Don't go borrowing just to impress that special one, if they really love and appreciate you they will appreciate whatever you get for them. It is not the cost of the gift but the heart from which it has come from.

Showing you appreciation should not be a one-off event, rather it should be a regular occurrence. It could be planned and also it could be spontaneous. Remember, the only way your partner would know you appreciate him or her is by saying it and showing it. It is important you match your words with your actions.

CHAPTER EIGHT

THE TIME

"What good are the greater things of life, if you cannot enjoy them with the one you love?"

Yes, I have such a poster hanging in my office to remind myself and my clients one of the benefits of being in a relationship. The moment you start a relationship with a person, you invariably made one decision; the decision to invest a great deal of your time with the partner you have found.

Do you remember when you first fell in love and started dating your partner? Let's go down memory lane... Do you remember how you could never seem to get enough of the person? There never seemed to be enough time in the world. When you were together it was as good as time no longer existed and when you were apart it seemed like time had been slowed. You could not wait to see each other and spend time together. You went everywhere together and did so many things together.

Uhmmm... seems like that was ages ago. Can you remember the last time you spent quality time with your partner? When was the last time you went to the movies together or went for a meal out or a drive together? It is little wonder that several months or years down the line, one complaint rises more and more above the rest. Increasing number of people is complaining that their partners barely spend any quality with them anymore.

When we chose to commit ourselves to someone, it means we have come to the realization of our lonely state and the need for a companion. Being in a relationship with another human being means willingness to share ourselves with them and this includes sharing out time with them. We have to realize that our lives aren't about us anymore and whatever decision we make, we have to include those we love as well.

Way too many people complain of how busy their partners are. They no longer have time for sharing a hug or a kiss or even sex have been reduced to just a quickie. Such a shame that many women are going to bed feeling lonely and hugging their pillows for comfort as their partners are not available to give them the comfort they need. Loneliness is increasingly becoming the cause of infidelity in many relationships today. Do you think this is because they no longer love each other?

Your guess is as good as mine. It is not because there is any love lost between the partners but rather each person or one partner gets caught up in the race of life. It so interesting to know that these things that often seek our attention and time are important but the truth is they are not as important as our human relationships.

When you love someone with your heart and deeply, you want to spend time with them. You want to see them, hug them and enjoy the allure of their scent when they are close to you. You want them to always be around when you need them.

Whenever I hear my clients say they do not have time to spend with their partners because of a very busy lifestyle, I grimace and immediately put my pad & pen down and look them straight in the eye. How do you justify not having time for the person you claim you love? How then, do you build a solid and stable relationship if you are too busy to spend time with your loved one?

Whenever I hear a spouse complain they cannot find the time, I just tell them then they will have all the time they need once they find themselves lonely. Human beings want intimacy and we can only get it with those of our kinds and whom our energy resonates with. I have seen certain people replace the love of man and woman with a pet and to me that is just absurd.

Many people often turn to substituting spending time with their partners with giving their partners gifts. The only problem with that is TIME can NEVER be SUBSTITUTED. Every good thing in life requires time to grow, for example, when you plant a flower it takes time to germinate and blossom. The process of growth cannot be fast tracked. Consider your career that you love so much, it took you time to develop, you went through the full process of getting educated and passing exams and probably you are in a profession that requires regular self-development. Why did you not offer gifts to your professors so they could pass you without you attending classes or sitting for your exams? Why did you commit so much time and effort to your work if you could possibly offer gifts to your bosses so you could be promoted? If you did not do this to build your career why do you think you can do this in your relationship? Little wonder many relationships are failing on this ground.

Let me state here, giving gifts in place of your time is a clear indication of guilt. You know you should spend more time with your partner but because you think you can get away with it you choose to appease your partner with gifts hoping they would accept your gifts in lieu of your time thus not giving them the grounds to complain.

A relationship is more than you giving your word of commitment to your partner. It is who you are. Your relationship can either make or break you. It is what you put into it that you get out of it. I will tell you of how making time is important in a relationship and how starting to do some things will definitely increase the quality of your relationship.

Remember it is about keeping the love, passion and romance in your relationship and you cannot do that when you are miles away from your partner.

Accepted that many jobs are very demanding and many of us are stuck in the conventional nine to five jobs and often doing overtime, worse still, taking work home with us.

I was speaking with a friend of mine, Alex, recently, he was lamenting on how hard it was becoming making his girlfriend happy. He reported she was always complaining and she never seemed satisfied with whatever he did for her. When I asked him what she complained mainly about, he reported that she had complained that he was never available and when he was available it was as good as he was not as he was always either on his phone or on the computer. He reported she complained that they never went anywhere together or do things together. Alex worked in an IT firm that required him working 9am to 5pm daily when he was on site and when he was off site these hours could be extended considerably. Apart from being in a tasking field, Alex also had a blog on the internet that required frequent updating which meant uncountable hours behind his computer when he got home. For someone with such a busy life, little wonder he has time to even be in a relationship.

Like every new relationship, when Alex started dating Melissa, they could hardly get enough of each other; they went everywhere together, did everything together and spent endless hours on the phone. As the weeks turned into months, the demand of Alex's job and his extracurricular activities began to have a toll on their relationship.

Poor Alex, he could not understand why his girlfriend could not be understanding and more supportive rather than adding to his problems.

I explained to Alex that his girlfriend was not trying to make things difficult but rather her incessant complaint was a desperate cry for his attention. I enquired from my friend when was the last time he spent quality time with her without having to rush off to do something else. Unfortunately, my friend could not give a definite answer; rather he still tried to justify his lack of time for his girlfriend.

I advised Alex to explain to his girlfriend the demands of his job and his blog as this would help her understand the pressure on him regarding work. I also advised him to help his girlfriend know that she was more important to him than his job and blog as no woman wants to feel that she is second best after work. I also advised him that if he wanted his relationship with Melissa to grow into something deeper and worth fighting for he needed to re-organize his life and actively create time for Melissa.

Ideally, work should not take us away from the ones that we love. My attitude to work basically is simple – No matter how irreplaceable my employers may make me feel, the truth still remains that if I die today another would fill my position by tomorrow – so the question is what is the point of sacrificing the only true thing that matter in life for that which does not.

Every human seeks companionship. The essence of every relationship is companionship and there is no way we can thrive if we do not make an effort to create time for companionship.

It's like trying to start a car on an empty tank or driving an electric powered car without the power source intact. If you decide to have a partner in your life, be ready to invest huge amounts of time into it. Even, if it means saying no to your bosses.

Managing time can be difficult for many people. It flies by so fast that we never even get to finish some of the tasks we have set out to do. I know it becomes more difficult when you are in a committed relationship as you are constantly pressed for time that you often do not seem to have.

I have outlined below ways you can turn things around and actually find that balance you have been looking for.

1. Purposely add your partner to your plans for the day and agree with your partner. Make sure this is something you and your partner can keep as the last thing you want is a 'no show' which can be disastrous to any relationship.

2. You can spend your journey time to work talking to your partner on the phone unless you are driving – this would not be advisable.

3. Purposely take your lunch break and make sure you leave your desk. If you can meet up with your partner for lunch or coffee, great! But if this is not possible spend that time talking to him or her on the phone. If you do talk on the phone, this is not the time to discuss serious stuff or argue but rather just gist.

4. At times, it could be a great idea to randomly send messages to your partner letting them know you love them and you are thinking about them. This often helps to let your partner know that though you are busy you still have them in mind.

5. Deliberately choose not to work overtime unless it is extremely important and you have a deadline that expires in 24 hours.

6. Deliberately leave work at work. Home is for relaxing. Home is for spending time with your loved ones. Don't

get home and head straight to the bedroom. Stay in the living room and relax with your partner.

7. Eat dinner together.
8. Watch TV together.
9. Go to bed together.
10. Spend time making love and not a quickie.
11. Make plans together.
12. Spend the weekends together and go on holidays together.
13. Try and create a set pattern during the day or night just for your partner such as talking to your partner on your way to and from work. You never know how much they would love and cherish these moments because they feel it is all about them then.
14. Hire a baby sitter if need be and go have fun with the love of your life.

As they say the quality of time matters more than the quantity. For me, I think I would say offer both quantity and quality in the same dose. You can have quality time alright but this could be 30 minutes which won't make much impact on the person you love if this is all they get in 1 week. But if you can have from as little as 2mins to even an hour daily for each other, you will be marvelled by the magnitude of improvement your relationship will have.

Don't make your goodbyes so abrupt or brief and without life, try and spend time holding hands, hugging and kissing.

Tell each other how much you both mean to one another and how much you will miss the other.

It seems quite a normal and simple thing but you have no idea how much impact it would have on your person. It makes the two of you feel connected, like you are members of same team.

Nurture the loving behaviour habits

Every love relationship starts with loving behaviours. Successful love relationship keeps and nurtures these habits. Loving habits can easily and gradually disappear in a relationship especially in marriage. So why not make it a habit to always treat your spouse the way you would want to be treated? Keep on the good loving habits in words and in actions. Spend quality time together.

Have a good laugh with your lover, share humour and jokes. Make your lover laugh.

Smile is the simplest expression with powerful effects. To create a lasting love relationship, you should have spent time having a good laugh together; make your lover laugh regularly. Bring some humour into your conversations and make your partner laugh.

WHEN BABY IS IN THE PICTURE

With babies come great responsibilities for both parents, and especially the mother who has to stay at home and take care of them. There is that common myth that when a baby comes, all the attention shifts to the child and the father is often an oblivious figure. Well, I cannot deny that this is what commonly happens in many homes but ideally, it should never be the case.

However, it depends on how you decide to approach the whole matter. As the husband, if you choose to help with the kids instead of letting mummy do all the work, it makes child care a lot easier. Look at it as the perfect time to catch up with your partner as diapers are changed, the babies are being fed or even when the babies are sleeping. When your partner begins to feel that you are part of the playing team and not a spectator standing at the line, she will appreciate you even more.

I have seen many couples fighting right after a baby comes into the picture. For the mother, she is overwhelmed with the task of nursing the baby and she needs all the help she can get from her husband, who probably is nowhere to be found. The husband on the other hand complains that his wife doesn't have time for him as all her time is consumed in child care.

I always advised that men should get involved. Child care is not a woman thing only. It requires the involvement of both parents. When a man helps his wife with taking care of the baby especially in the night time and weekends when he is available, this helps take away pressure from the woman and she feels less stressed and has time for herself and she is then able to spend quality time with her man. Sharing child care between parents increases the bond between man and woman and also between parents and child.

CHAPTER NINE

THE TOUCH

TOUCHING AND HOLDING HANDS

$\mathscr{T}$ouching is a physical sign of love, romance and passion in a relationship. To create a lasting romantic relationship you need to cultivate the habit of hand holding, touching and hugging your partner many times daily. There are no rules to how many times in a day you should hold hands but as often as possible; hold hands when walking, hold hands when standing or waiting. When you are fond of holding your partner's hand spontaneously every time you are walking together says to your partner that you are madly in love with him or her.

Nicki and Pedro have been together for 3 years but Nicki was always complaining that she did not think Pedro was in love with her. I could not understand this as they both seemed happy together. Pedro believed that Nicki was his world and he could not survive without her. If this was the case, why then did Nicki feel Pedro was not in love with her? After several talk with Nicki and Pedro I discovered where the confusion was coming from. TOUCH.

Yes, you heard me right. TOUCH. Nicki was the 'touch' person while Pedro was not.

Touch is very important and essential in every relationship. Any relationship that has a lot of touching tends to last long.

Nicki wanted Pedro to express his love beyond words and a simple kiss. She wanted a display of affection, she wanted to feel loved and wanted all at once. She wanted her man to make her feel alive and like a woman, but Pedro was a dead knob at this bit. In fact, when in public, Pedro was always so shy that he would walk a slight distance away from his lover. Sounds awkward to the ear but I understand Pedro's condition a bit.

Not all of us are comfortable with touching and public display of affection.

This special section is dedicated to all those special dead knobs that need a few tips on how to speak a thousand words without actually saying a word.

Research has shown that touch is very vital for the survival of any baby and it is said that how you handle your baby right from infancy to when they grow up can greatly influence the kind of person they become.

Infants respond pretty well to touch as it is a sign of love from their parents. If this loving touch is continued throughout the child's early years, these kids often grow up happy and self-confident. They find it easier to express their feelings verbally and non-verbally.

Pedro unfortunately, had grown up in an environment where there was no touching. He could not remember his parents or siblings hugging him or giving him a warm pat on the shoulder. He had grown up feeling embarrassed about touching.

It should also be noted that our culture and background greatly influences how we feel about touching. Some cultures embrace touching while some cultures frown against it.

Regardless of what culture we have grown up in, it is important to understand the love language of your partner and speak to them as they would understand. It is of no use saying "I am not a touch person" like Pedro. If your partner is a touch person then you need to learn to communicate to him /her this way.

There are different types of touching and each one expresses a different emotion. For the purpose of this book I would keep it limited to the touch that promotes love, romance and passion. Let me state here that hitting, kicking, punching, pinching, pushing, pulling, slapping, striking and strangling are forms of touching that can never communicate love, romance and passion. A touch that incites fear and intimidation does not promote a healthy relationship. Regardless of how much love the perpetrator claims to have for you. Love and violence do not go hand in hand. These forms of touching are classified as PHYSICAL ABUSE. No one should stay in an abusive relationship. You are better and worth more than that.

Touch communicates a lot and you want to make sure that you are passing across the right message when you touch your partner. For those who are used to touching this is second nature but for the people like Pedro, who need to learn the art of touching, you want to make sure you get it right. Admitted, you will feel very awkward initially but with constant use, gradually, the art is developed and you are able to speak a thousand words without using verbal language but the use of touch.

In any committed relationship, there are two types of touching that promotes love, romance and passion – sexual touch and non-sexual touch. In the pages ahead, I would be looking in depth into these two types of touch.

Don't stop curdling up together

When you are in bed, take some time curdling before you sleep, one great way to curdle is to lie on your side you're your body shaped like the letter "S". Often with the man behind but that's not a rule. Just stay close to your partner and let your bodies fix together like to spoons and enjoy the warmth and security you feel.

It's OK if you hold on to each other until you both sleep off, it will definitely be a great night and a refreshing morning.

Don't stop touching when outside

Touching nicking and pecking should be regular and genuine way of telling your lover that you notice and appreciate their body and presence. As much as possible have physical body contact every time you are together.

CHAPTER TEN

THE GIFTS

G iving gifts unconditionally to people around us is not necessarily simple and giving in a love relationship is not that simple either, although the need to express our feelings can sometimes make giving in a relationship less tasking. When giving gifts to your partner feels like a chore, resentment is likely to be developed towards your partner, when this happens perhaps it is time to check if the love is still truly where it used to be, because love gives unconditionally.

In some relationships, partners give gifts to their loved ones in order to get something in return or to satisfy their ego, or sometimes to distract the partner from current unpleasant situation. When we give gifts in this light we are only giving to get 'a narcissistic hit' as described by Daniel Goleman.

We all knew that true love gives unconditionally, but how can we learn to give gifts without strings attached when we are accustomed to feeling either a sense of duty, or we want gratitude from others in return? The simple answer is we must first learn to share before we can truly learn to give. Unconditional gift-giving starts by sharing a piece of yourself - your love or esteem and care for your partner shown by the time taken to select a gift in a considerate manner, and combining this with a heart of gratitude for who your partner is and not wanting anything at all in return.

7 WAYS TO GIVE GIFTS

1. Give with a Meaning:

Find a gift that means something about the other person to you and be proud of whatever gift you choose. Buying a gift because it is on sale or bargain or even because it is the most expensive item in the store will not give meaning to your gift. Put effort, care and consideration into the purchase or creation of the gift. It is often best to make the gift like it is a 'piece of you' to your partner.

2. Give with a surprise.

We all know that a gift prompted by persistent requests for it is not as exciting or fulfilling as a gift that is a total surprise. This does not mean that you cannot give to meet the obvious needs of your partner, but you should think ahead to figure out what your partner would need by been observant and knowing them, rather than heeding direct requests for items or gifts from your partner. One example is giving a voucher for a massage, spa treatment at weekend because your partner has had a long week at work.

3. Give Carefully:

You should think carefully about what your partner would not buy for themselves probably for financial reasons or time. If you give items that your partner is already very adept at getting for themselves, he/she may see this as an invasion of that territory and they may feel you' re trying to substitute their sense of style with yours. Since you already know what your partner does well, don't even bother. Instead look for the things they'd never consider buying - like the red or brown designer bag you overheard them pondering about but muttered that they couldn't afford, or a meal they have never tried before in a new restaurant.

4. Give room for a change of Mind;

You should let your partner know in a gentle way that if they do not like the gift or they prefer a different colour or style, that your gift can be returned for a refund or for an exchange, re-gifted, or donated if it doesn't make them feel comfortable or happy. You do not want to create a noose around their necks. I remember as a child, when a family member would give my mum some gift that she considered hideous and would keep it out of sight. Most times when the named family member comes visiting, she would have ensured the gift was on full view. I have learnt that the sense of obligation can turn gift-receiving into a burden rather than a delight.

5. Give non general gifts:

By general gifts I mean a gift that you give to your partner but the entire household can use it. For example, a pressing iron, toaster, blender etc. Avoid giving such "useful" items to your partner that you know will end up been used by the whole household. These things do service for everyone and are not gifts in the usual sense. Such gifts do not say something about you to the person. They do not tell you something special about your partner.

6. Give Without expecting Reciprocation

Every time you give to your partner, you are giving because you want to. If you don't want to, then you need to reassess the point of what it is that you are really doing. Do not expect gratitude, smiles or something in return. Although most respectful and well-mannered people will demonstrate gratitude, and it's almost certain that your partner would be grateful for your gifts, but there are times where this will not be forthcoming for one reason or other but that does not necessarily mean that your partner doesn't respect your gift-giving or not appreciate it. Sometimes men are embarrassed, too surprised, shy, ashamed, or self-conscious to react in a gracious manner. What matters is that you have given with a good heart, your partner's reaction or lack of one should not bother you. If you look deeper, you will see truly how the gift has been received.

7. Give with Style:

Present you gift well, sometimes the wrapping of the gift may mean a lot to your partner, than the gift inside. Because it shows your sense of style, how much effort you've put into the presentation and it is a demonstration of respect for the partner. It doesn't have to be complex, or expensive, just put effort to have a great presentation.

Give some pleasant surprises

A successful love relationship is not boring, or predictable. Give your lover some little pleasant surprises every now and again, don't overdo it, don't be predictable, introduce varieties to what you do, what you say, what you give, how you do it, how you say it and where you do and say it.

Variety is the spice of life, so also is variety the spice for a lasting love relationship. You will grow loving romantic sparks in your love life when you introduce in some pleasant surprises.

CHAPTER ELEVEN

THE MONEY

How to handle Money in a Love Relationship & Marriage

*M*ost times engaged couples and newly met lovers are able to easily figure out the best wedding reception, which colour theme and the photographer to use, but they can't seem to bring up the topic of their finances – a crucial issue that could make or break their marriage.

Money is the leading source of disagreement for couples, whether they're just hitched or have been married for decades, and in extreme cases, tensions around household finances can even lead to divorce.

The best way to avoid the money mistake in relationship is to have serious discussions about your finances long before you go too far into the relationship or long before you say 'I do'.

Discuss all aspect of your finance with your partner, everything from current income and debts to attitudes towards money spending and saving for retirement. These days, many newlyweds enter into marriage with piles of student loan or credit card debt, it's definitely important to talk about it.

In a recent survey by the National Foundation for Credit Counselling, nearly 70% of adults said they had negative feelings about discussing money with a fiancé, while more than 20% said the discussion would lead to a fight, reveal unknown financial issues or even cause them to break off the engagement.

According to Dr. Terri Orbuch, a social psychologist and author of '5 Simple Steps to Take Your Marriage from Good to Great' - many people simply haven't learned how to talk about money with others.

The way people were raised often time influence the way they deal with money. For instance, a young adult who has an allowance or opened a savings account may grow up sticking to a budget and may be more used to saving some money for later, while a child who grows up receiving gifts including cash may view spending as a way to show love and appreciation.

When you identify your differences in the way you approach finances, you will be able to set ground rules that will merge your approaches. Let me give you some of the examples you may relate to; a spender who is in relationship with a saver will have to learn how to put some money aside for saving and to stick to budget. A lady who is an impulsive shopper will have to learn to be more cautious in spending when in relationship with a man who is more deliberate about big-ticket spending.

Here are some of the tips I give to some of the couples I have counselled.

1. **Stay Calm when you discuss money with your partner:** It's counterproductive when you ambush your partner with a money talk. Be clever and be careful about when you raise the topic. Look for a more relaxed atmosphere with less stress, when your partner will be more receptive and understanding. .

2. **Don't hide any financial information:** Honesty is very important when you discuss money, don't hide any income or debt from your partner; it will only lead to a bigger problem in the future.

3. **Be detailed about your discussion.** Do your research before approaching your partner; find many ways to merge your different approaches to finances. Give fact and figures that are practicable and achievable. Suggest real life workable financial plans.

4. **Talk about family.** From loaning money to a sibling to caring for aging parents, you and your partner should be on the same page with how you will approach these types of situations.

5. **Don't stop talking about finances:** Don't just talk about finances when times are tough, review your past discussion and agreement. Do not set any rule on stone; no one wants to live their lives in a relationship being subjected to financial rules that cannot be altered. Times do change; things can get better, as your financial situations change see how you can adjust your past spending arrangements.

If your partner is over spending

Deborah Price, author of *The Heart of Money: A Couple's Guide to Creating True Financial Intimacy* puts it that

"Money is an area where we're prone to being irrational, illogical, and overly emotional."

You must tread gently when you want to tackle your partner over spending habit.

If your partner is a spendthrift, follow these ground rules to tackle the issue

Impeccable timing: As I mentioned previously, the number one rule is good timing; Choose a time when you're both relaxed, less stressed, and in a good mood like a weekend morning, and make sure you each have at least half an hour free to be able to discuss the matter in detail.

Don't give accusations: You must avoid the use of sentences like "You did"; focus on "We." Let your partner know the issue is concern for both of you and as a team you must tackle the problem before it gets out of hands.

Avoid using the word 'Budget', 'Cut' We all know the word budget or cut or cut back has negative connotations and every time we hear the words, they paint a picture of impending discomfort or pain. Instead use words like spending plan, spending considerations, non-essential spending etc. these terms are more likely to resonate with a spendthrift.

Regular review: You will see great results if you review and repeat these talks regularly. You can schedule a monthly review to track improvements with spending on both sides.

THE BEST APPROACH TO TACKLE MONEY ISSUES WITH YOUR PARTNER

Real Life Practical Examples:

The experts have advised using this approach to talk to your partner on the issue of money:

1. Opening trick: say something like "I'm feeling a little stressed about money. Now that the holidays are over, I'm worried we may have spent too much. Can we talk about our financial plans?"

Tip: The great thing about this strategy is that it opens up the conversation by saying how you're felling not about what your partner has done.

In most cases, your partner is more likely to respond positively. Your partner is likely to feel sorry for causing you discomfort and would be more inclined to apologize than being defensive.

2. Take part of the responsibility: you can say something like "I know that gym membership club I joined set our finance back quite a bit."

Tip: When you use this strategy, your partner will feel less defensive since you are taking part of the blame for your financial situation. Your partner will be open to discuss with you as a team rather than being defensive. Even if you can't see any reason to take part of the blame, look for other ways you may have contributed to the situation. Remember, no one is prefect, and there are things that we do that our partners are not happy about either.

3. Take the bull by the horn: start by saying "I love you, and I didn't mean to make you angry. How can we talk about this without getting into trouble with each other?"

Tip: we all know the subject of money itself is enough to raise hackles, but when you start by asking for the best way to approach it, your partner will be more likely to be interested in the conversation and the tension will be far less.

4. Quote some details in context: you can say something like "I ran the numbers. If we keep spending this way, it will take us another five years until we can afford the kind of house we want."

Tip: according to Peterson; "Putting the overspending in the context of the greater picture is more effective than being nit-picky". "When you bring the focus back to your joint values and goals, your partner will be more receptive."

5. Pass the baton to your partner: you can say this "We got into a jam this time. How do you think we can avoid it in the future?"

Tip: this trick makes you give control over to the person who is at fault. Your partner will be more likely to accept responsibility for the situation.

Your partner will feel like you are a great team when you discuss any major spending. Discussing with your partner and sleeping over it often helps you see how unnecessary some purchases can be. As a rule, never make a major purchase that will eat major part of your finance without discussing with your spouse.

CHAPTER TWELVE

REAL LIFE CASES STUDIES

MONEY AND MARRIAGE

*B*efore we dive into the real life case studies, let me first make it clear that there's no right way for married couples or partners to manage their money. But there are plenty of wrong ways. According to John Thyden, a prominent Washington, D.C., divorce attorney "Financial issues are the primary reason for 90 percent of divorce cases I handle, but it isn't necessarily the amount of money a couple has that tends to trip them up. It's the differences in their spending habits and especially their lack of communication."

However, as you will see in the case studies and real life profiles of these couples I will be discussing here, husbands and wives, partners in love relationships with differing financial habits and attitudes can make things work — if they're willing to be honest with each other and to reach compromise on money issue. Carol and I definitely have our share of conflicts over finances, but we deal with them in a respectful way.

These couples below are featured in Money.CNN.com and GoodHouseKeeping.com under the news on marriage and money. I have chosen them because their situations are very similar to those that I have worked with over the years. You will see how each of these couples ran into money mistakes in their relationships and how they found smart solutions to overcome their money issues. Their clever techniques may work for you too.

<u>Couple</u>: The Maidenbergs

Picking their battles:

Michelle, 37, a psychotherapist, spends money much more readily than her husband, Eric, 38, a banker. Case in point: a planned addition and renovations to their house in New Rochelle, NY, a home that they share with their three young sons, 7, 4, and 2.

For a year, Michelle has urged Eric to agree on taking step one: hiring an architect to sketch the plans, at a cost of $30,000. But Eric, a self-described "calculated decision maker," refuses to commit a cent until he learns the amount of his annual bonus: "I'm not willing to say yes until we know we'll have the money to do the work."

That's an impasse that could've led to fighting — but in the Maidenbergs' case, it didn't. Even though she and her husband are on different timetables, Michelle is confident the project will get done, so she's willing to postpone until Eric is more comfortable. That kind of ebb-and-flow approach has worked well for them. Says Michelle: "If I sense Eric will give in when he feels more comfortable about the cost, I don't argue; I just wait him out."

In other situations, she compromises to get her way — as in a skirmish, during her most recent pregnancy, at a maternity-clothing store. "In my first trimester, I really needed some items to help me transition from regular things to pregnancy clothes. When we got to the cashier, the total was several hundred dollars and I could tell Eric was annoyed (partly at the price, and partly because it had taken me over an hour to find things I liked).

So I suggested the clothes be his birthday present to me. Basically, I traded a future gift for clothes I felt I needed — and it worked! He paid with a smile and even gave me a kiss, saying, 'Happy birthday!' And I never heard about it afterward."

The Maidenbergs say if you're half of a couple where well-intentioned caution can slow money decisions to a crawl, the secret is sensitivity. "If there's something I want, I speak Eric's language," says Michelle. "That means using logic and pointing out the costs and benefits, so he sees that a purchase does make sense for us."

Source: GoodHouseKeeping.com

Couple: The Charests

Learning to complement each other:

Many couples have a spender and a saver. But Bob and Cindy Charest of Westbrook, ME, are partners in a band, and blend approaches into one harmonious style.

Their money partnership goes like this: A penny-pincher who loves to splurge (Cindy) is married to a free spender with a knack for saving on large expenses and keeping finances on track (Bob). Says Cindy: "I save first, and then spend; Bob spends first, and then saves."

Cindy, 52, known to friends as "Save-a-Buck Cin," comes by the nickname honestly: "I'm constantly turning lights off around the house." But piling up the pennies doesn't preclude a love for extravagances, like a recent European trip with children Leigh, 18, and Mark, 15.

Bob, 55, tends to spend small and often. And while he'd probably ignore the penny on the street, Bob is cautious about serious outlays. Example: A boiler company estimated it would cost $3,000 to repair their furnace. Bob grabbed a wrench, researched the job, and did it himself for a sliver of the estimate.

The formula generally works because the Charests know it can. So Bob and Cindy defer to each other's money strengths. Bob knows Cindy's thriftiness helps make the family's blowouts possible. Cindy applauds Bob's eye for the larger financial picture: "I'm a horrible money manager, so I willingly delegate that job to Bob," she says. "If I were paying the bills, we'd be in jail."

Source: GoodHouseKeeping.com

Couple: The Geigers

Letting the best money manager manage the money:

Before Jan Dahlin Geiger and her husband, Jerry, of Atlanta got married 15 years ago — each for the second time — they were financial opposites. Jan Dahlin, 58, a financial planner, was debt averse. "I was saving 10 percent for retirement and my kids' college fund and did not have a cent of debt, other than a $50,000 mortgage," she says. By his own admission, Jerry, 66, a sales executive, earned a lot and spent a lot. With his shiny cars, a divorce that cost him six figures, and more than $10,000 in credit card and other debt, he was deep in the red. "It was an addiction," he says. "I got into the habit of spending whatever I had. I had to borrow money, because I was spending in anticipation of making it." Jan Dahlin sums it up: "He spent money like a wild man."

And she was horrified. Through her work, Jan Dahlin had seen many people's lives ruined by financial recklessness. "My first response was, 'I can't marry him,'" she says. "I told him if he wanted to marry me, we needed to make hard choices."

Realizing he had to either change or remain single, Jerry sat down and discussed finances with Jan Dahlin. Then he agreed to a comprehensive money overhaul, including:

Paying down his debts: Some $110,000 in loans and credit card interest was erased in two years.

Not keeping up with the Joneses: The Geigers agreed to buy a $200,000 home rather than the half-million-dollar one Jerry craved.

Other trade-downs: Gone are the BMWs and Cadillacs. Now he tools around in a used Dodge minivan.

Monthly reviews: To track their financial progress.

Jerry concedes that changing his ways wasn't easy: "It was like shock treatment. I remember how I struggled to come to terms with the less expensive house." But when he retires at 67, "we'll be able to take an awesome vacation every month if we want to," says Jan Dahlin. "I can honestly say we have had few fights over money. And our net worth today is about 1,000 percent of what it was 15 years ago."

Source: GoodHouseKeeping.com

Too much debt

COURTESY: DEACON HAYES

<u>Couple</u>: **Deacon and Kim Hayes**

<u>Relationship status</u>: **Married five years**

City: Phoenix, Ariz.

Shortly after their 2008 wedding, Deacon and Kim Hayes sat down to assess their finances. The couple was shocked to discover that between the two of them, they had more than $50,000 in debt and two mortgages.

Between student loans, an auto loan for a brand-new Nissan Altima and about $7,000 in credit card debt, their outstanding debt added up to $52,000. And that didn't include the two mortgages Deacon had inked in 2006 before their marriage, one for the condo they lived in and one an investment property.

So the couple took action. They cut all of the extras: out went their cable subscription, a gym membership and eating out. Most importantly, they sold the new car, along with an older car, and replaced them with two used cars that they bought for about $5,000. The cuts freed up hundreds of dollars a month to pay down their debt.

Despite all the money saving moves, Hayes foreclosed on the property that he had been renting out in 2010. He now realizes the home was the opposite of a great investment.

In the same year, however, the couple managed to pay down all of their non-mortgage related debt. At first, "we didn't really see the light at the end of the tunnel," Deacon said. "It was overwhelming. There was tension. But it was a catalyst for us to start making some drastic changes."

Source: Money.CNN.com

Wrong money decision

COURTESY: DAVID SAUCEDO

<u>Couple</u>: David Saucedo and Mariana Terrezas
<u>Relationship status</u>: Engaged

City: El Paso, Texas

After almost five years of working as a tax accountant, David Saucedo had succumbed to major "corporate burnout."

He quit his job, opting instead to work for the family locksmithing business. While he was thrilled to be out of corporate America, his decision also meant a major salary cut -- and limiting the financial options for him and his soon-to-be wife.

"I put my happiness above the financial stability that I could have brought into the marriage," he said. "So right now, things are a little tough."

Combined with a recent car loan his fiancée took out, his new salary has made the couple's goal to qualify for a mortgage more difficult than they had expected. While Saucedo said he doesn't regret his decision, he wishes he had timed his move a bit differently.

"In hindsight, I should have closed on a house with my old job," he said. "I just wasn't thinking clearly."

Source: Money.CNN.com

A bad investment

COURTESY: RACHELE BOUCHAND

<u>Couple</u>: **Rachele and Blaise Bouchand**

<u>Relationship status</u>: **Newlyweds**

City: Bellevue, Wash.

Even financial planners can make mistakes with their money.

When Rachele Bouchand was dating her now-husband Blaise, he asked her to take a look at the small individual retirement account that a friend had helped him open in 2011. But Bouchand put it off, assuming that the investment was fine.

When she finally looked at the account three months ago, she discovered his $6,000 had been invested in a gold and commodities fund that came with high fees and had lost money, even as stocks soared.

While a basic stock fund would likely have returned major gains, his investment had sunk to around $4,000, she said. They have since moved the account, and Bouchand gave her husband advice she usually gives her clients.

"I gave my husband a mini-lesson on asset allocation and fees," she said. "I was so embarrassed and angry that this happened in my own household."

Source: Money.CNN.com

No emergency savings

COURTESY: CHRIS MILES

Couple: Chris and Lyndsie Miles

Relationship status: Married 11 years

City: Salt Lake City, Utah

In the mid-2000s, things were good for the Miles family. But when the recession hit and Chris' investment advisory business faltered, the couple started hemorrhaging cash.

They were spending thousands more a month than Chris's small business was taking in. The couple lost nearly everything, including a Mercedes and their home, which the bank foreclosed on in 2009, a week after their fourth child was born.

Now that the family has gotten their spending in check, Chris says they have learned the importance of emergency savings and not relying on their home as a possible source of quick money.

"The biggest lesson we learned was to not be overly optimistic, arrogant and foolish with our money," Chris Miles said.

Source: Money.CNN.com

Avoided money talks

COURTESY: SONITA LONTOH

Couple: Sonita Lontoh and Adam Skarsgard

Relationship status: Married 12 years

City: San Francisco, Calif.

Sonita Lontoh and her husband Adam Skarsgard have starkly contrasting money habits. Lontoh, for example, loves splurging on designer shoes and clothing purchases, while Skarsgard prefers to save for big sporting events, like the Super Bowl or Kentucky Derby.

In their first years of marriage, Lontoh said she avoided serious money talks, preferring instead to keep a wall between them and their finances.

"For me, money is a symbol of my independence so having to make decisions with someone else took a while for me to get used," Lontoh said.

The couple has since learned to communicate, and now agree on a budget that works for them both. "It's actually much better for the marriage," she said.

Source: Money.CNN.com

Reference

http://money.cnn.com/gallery/news/2013/07/18/marriage-money/index.html

http://www.goodhousekeeping.com/family/budget/marriage-money-issues

10 QUICK AND EASY WAYS TO BRING BACKTHE SPARKS AND THE BUTTERFLIES IN YOUR SELF AND YOUR PARTNER

1. Bear One another's Burden

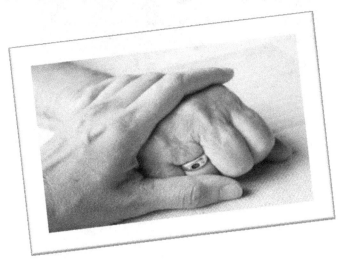

*B*ear one another's burdens; every relationship comes with some form of burden that comes from each or both partners. Learn to sense when your spouse needs help, even when he or she does not ask for it. When helpfulness becomes such a matter of habit in your relationship, two lovers will feel and act like a winning team.

2. Reach compromise on Issues

Great couples reach compromise all the time. Sometimes you may have to agree to disagree but you should always come to an agreement. This is a part of any successful marriage. No one should insist on having things done their way all the time.

3. Cheer up your partner always

You should be the number one cheerleader for your partner. The support you give your partner in any way would make them feel very important. In any way you can encourage and cheer up your lover.

4. Help your partner to keep fit and healthy

To have a long lasting love relationship you need to be in good health as good health is required to live 'till death do us part'.

Do not neglect the health of your partner, involve your partner in any exercise regime, if possible use the gym together, spend time working out together, and practise health habits together. It's been proven that exercising with a partner is highly encouraging and motivating.

If your partner is taking any medication encourage him or her to stick to their prescriptions. Also you can go to annual physicals, and get enough sleep and exercise.

5. Make love

Create time to have more great sex (aka make love)! But be spontaneous, you can have it during the day instead of at night or if you two are home alone. Taking sex out of the bedroom can give a different experience and pleasure.

6. Don't stop greeting with a kiss

It is very important to kiss every time you leave or come together, no matter how busy, no matter where you are, when leaving or when coming together, it's a great sign you still have strong attraction and spark for your lover. Don't allow the passage of time to erode your passion. Make your reunion very passionate and warm.

7. Don't stop sharing your money with your lover

Stinginess has no place in a successive marriage and love relationship. Share your money with your partner, it does not mean that you have to put all your money into one bank account, it is great for both to know what bills you are paying, and the outstanding financial commitments. When your lover is financially in need, give, if for any reason there is not sufficient money to meet the need at hand, talk about it and let your partner know you care, see what you can do to work around the need. It will go a long way to assure your partner that you care and make a commitment to be there in every situation.

8. Send sexy romantic messages

You should send love messages to your partner regularly during the day, thanks to mobile technology and internet; you can send romantic texts at any time to your partner.

Send your love messages through more than one media, send through Facebook, texts, emails, and send cards, write a few words and post to your partner's work address.

Send it when your partner least expects it. You will create a great spark and romance in your relationship.

Taking the time to put into words how much your spouse means to you is the greatest of gifts you can give any time any day.

9. Let your partner have freedom to be

It's very vital that you let your partner be him or herself, we are all complex human being with unique desires and interests, needs and desires. Respect the individuality of your spouse. Have your time alone to build your mind and spirit. Do not get jealous or angry when the person you love needs to be alone. To have a lasting love relationship, each lover must respect the alone time from each other. After all time alone is a fundamental predisposition of every human being.

10. Eat well, eat healthily and eat together

Eat together, when its possible, go out for a meal occasionally, help your lover to eat healthy and if your partner already has bad eating habits, help him or her to overcome the bad eating habits. Have lovely conversations over a meal.

FINAL WORD

*W*hen we were little boys and girls we were taught and believe that there is a "Price Charming" or "Knight in Shining Armour" that will one day come in and sweep us off our feet. And we innocently believed that the "Frog" can be turned into that Prince with just the touch of our lips. When we became adults we soon discovered the imperfection in men and women. Most men built the wrong image of who they want as lover in their heads; they imagine every woman should be June Cleaver combined with the sex-appeal of Marilyn Monroe, but unfortunately this if far from the reality

When things go wrong in our marriage, the world we live in now a days suggests to us that our partner does not measure up to our expectations and most couples will give up before they even consider looking into the issue. We somehow forget all the wonderful qualities this person had that caused us to marry him or her in the first place, and we begin analysing and picking apart all of their weaknesses and imperfections.

But if you loved that person enough to marry them, then you can find it in yourself to love them enough to continue to fight for them and help bring out the best in them rather than expect them to just bring out the best in you.

I hope I have been able to bless you from my knowledge and real life experience. I do not claim to be perfect or know it all but I strive to put in my best to bring out the best in my partner. I believe we can bring back the sparks, the butterflies and the stutters in any marriage or love relationship where there is none left. We have gone through all the real life case studies, real life situation and examples of couples who have fought through to happy romantic and rewarding love relationships. It still remains for you to take action and I hope you will give it your best, starting right now

I wrote this book for you, I sincerely hope it changes your relationship and if you find the information in this book helpful, please give it to someone. It would be my greatest pleasure if you would give a copy of this book to your family members, friends, relatives, colleagues, church members, and every one you think would be blessed by the information in this book. I hope all you dreams of happy, romantic and rewarding love relationship come true sooner than you think.

Thanks For Reading My Book and Feel Free To Get in Touch with Me

Paulmclovett@BringBackTheSparks.com

www.Facebook.com/BringBackTheSparks

ACKNOWLEDGMENT

I am indebted to many professionals who have been of great help to me in writing, editing and publishing this book to meet publication deadline. A million thanks to Lynda Vincent, Dr. Jay Polma, and Professor Rana K WIlliam for all your contributions to this great work. Thank you.

I appreciate all the great couples I have worked with in my carrier who gave me permission to tell their stories to change the lives of others. This book is a tribute to your sincerity and honesty.

My concept of love, passion and romance in marriage was shaped by great marriage counsellors, relationship experts and incredible authors. I acknowledge and appreciate Dr. Gary Chapman whose works have given me great insights over the years, I appreciate Dr. John M. Gottman, Gary Thomas, Bishop Luke Roland, Bishop John Francis, and other great messengers of love and restoration.

And lastly, I appreciate all those who will tread this book and make a decision to work on their relationship to restore all that was lost, and bring back the magic and the sparks to create a lasting rewarding relationship. I love you all.

ABOUT THE AUTHOR

Paul McLovett is a relationship coach, author and marriage counsellor, he works with couples locally and travels across countries sharing the message of restoration to bring back or re-energize love, passion, romance in marriage and all love relationships.

You can reach through his email and Facebook.

Paulmclovett@BringBackTheSparks.com

www.Facebook.com/BringBackTheSparks

INDEX

CPSIA information can be obtained
at www.ICGtesting.com
Printed in the USA
FSHW01n0906260518
48726FS